The Euro is Dead; Long live the Solid!

Eduardo J. Belgrano

DEDICATION

To Pavla, Eddie, Olivia and Klara.

CONTENTS

PREFACE

This booklet addresses the question, "how can we provide a feasible, long- term solution for the current serious problem troubling all Eurozone member countries?" the author contends that this will be hardly achieved by traditional mainstream economics recipes, not only because these have in the past proved to be mere "patches" providing short- term solutions, but because in this particular case, there is another new element nonexistent within previous fiat money environments. we refer to the element of sovereignty. the author contends that this is the fatal flaw of the euro monetary system, which was conceived by politicians in search of a legacy, and by mainstream economists advising them, who did not realize the flaw or decided to sweep it under the rug.

Amazingly, politicians in relatively economically strong countries are proposing to solve the problem by taking away yet more sovereignty from country members, in order to impose economic measures to governments in those countries suffering from acute recessionary forces.

Aware of the limits and deficiencies wrought by government controlled money as well as the particular political challenges presented by having one sole currency spanning many independent countries in Europe, the author puts forth a proposal involving the issuance of a new supranational currency backed by a 100 percent gold reserve, circulating side- by- side with the local re-issued currencies (DM, Franc, Drachma, etc.) at variable rates of exchange.

The author explains how the DLCCS-dual level currency competition system he proposes addresses the need some countries have to act asymmetrically vis- a- vis other Eurozone members, from an economic point of view. He explains further that this will allow any Eurozone country member to set its own economic policy independently from Brussels, without wrecking havoc in the Eurozone.

The website for this booklet is: www.TheEuroIsDeadBooklet.com.

ACKNOWLEDGMENTS

In this section authors normally express their thanks to some people without whose help and support the book would not have been possible. I would have liked at least to have had the time to ask third parties to review this short manuscript. Regretfully, there was no time due to the fact that I wanted to have this booklet published as soon as possible to maintain its relevance vis a vis the situation in the Eurozone.

Notwithstanding this, I do have some acknowledgments to make, albeit of a different nature to people who however are all dead, their ideas will live forever. First of all, I wish to express my gratitude to Richard Cantillon, the founder of political economy who in the 18th Century presented a brilliant contribution on monetary theory, the business cycle and the role of the entrepreneur in the economy. Deepest gratitude are also due to Adam Smith, David Ricardo, and all the extraordinary developers of the capital-based macroeconomic theory, such as, Carl Menger, Eugen Böhm-Bawerk, Ludwig v. Mises and F.A. Hayek to name a few. The author would also like to express his respect of Karl Marx, paragon of socialism who brought into the spotlight the dreadful plight of workers during the industrial revolution. It is also stupefying the fact that at the same time as failing to understand human nature, he borrowed from Ricardo and concocted a theory of value bordering on the absurd which notwithstanding conquered the minds of millions, setting back the economic development of some countries and the wellness of its people for a great number of years to come.

INTRODUCTION

"Never have so many been fooled, for so long, by so few"
Eduardo Belgrano

The proposal to create a renaissance in the Eurozone which I describe here in this short monograph is not one to which "mainstream  economists" will warm up. I hardly expect it to be seriously considered as a solution to the euro muddle, not because it is not a good solution, but because it goes against economic tenets rabidly upheld by the ruling class in the Eurozone, however wrong and misguided these tenets are. The mere thought of introducing a 100 percent reserve gold currency such as the new supranational money I am proposing should be enough to cause any mainstream economist a severe case of intellectual apoplexy.

Mediocre politicians seeking to leave a legacy with the help of enabling mainstream economists originally created the failed euro concept. Mainstream economists have also utterly failed in our time in their quest to find a solution to the current mess, which was unquestionably bound to happen. It would seem they would rather see the Eurozone descend into Dante's inferno and chaos, than introduce a real long-term solution, albeit outside their cherished mainstream economic theories.

Monetary systems, such as those based on the gold standard or any other system related to them, are a definitive no-no to mainstream economists. During the time I studied economics in Germany and in the course of my research work I used to visit quite often two of the five government economic think tanks. One friend of mine, a researcher at one of these government institutions, told me in unequivocal terms that he believed in what is known as the Austrian school of economics, but would never even entertain the notion of stating so much in front of anyone at the institute. He added further that doing so could lead to being ostracized and even to the loss of his job. Economic theories dissonant to the mainstream order are not very well tolerated; intellectual Hobbesian hells are alive, well and kicking.

The main objective of writing this booklet is to inform those suffering from the "slings and arrows" wrought by the failed concept of the Euro, that there is indeed a solution to their plight, albeit not easily enacted. To start with, it would require the concerted effort of the population of most Eurozone country members to vote out of office the failed politicians running the show.

The Euro has proved to be a failure as it has neither fulfilled the long-term expectations of the founders of the system nor of those of the politicians who currently continue to believe it can still succeed. The Euro is a dead proposition which was bound to fail from the very beginning, due to the fact that Europe is made up of different countries with different governments and very different economies hence, having different needs at different times. The much talked about economic "Convergence" as a condition all members would have to adhere to was, still is and will forever be an utterly utopian concept, as unrealistic as is to think that the creation of the United Nations would prevent the occurrence of wars. The Euro currency was and is a sort of procrustean bed proposition dictated by Brussels acting as some sort of *Damastes*, compelling victims of all sizes (read Euro members) to fit in his "economic convergence" iron bed.

In this essay we will argue that to save it –irrespective of any country leaving the unique currency system- the current Euro currency system should be converted into a monetary system based along the lines of the currency competition theory proposed by Professor Friedrich Hayek[1]. We have refined the concept and proposed in previous papers a monetary system based on one gold currency competing with local currencies which we call the "Dual Level Currency Competition System," and have been advocating it since the early 1980s, writing articles in various publications in different countries. In essence, we propose to exchange the Euro for a gold-backed currency and have all members of the Eurozone reissue their own currencies which would compete with the new money which we will call "Solid" and also compete between themselves; both currencies will have legal tender status. Thus the Solid would circulate in all countries of the Eurozone as well as the local currencies at variable exchange rates depending on demand, essentially based on the international price of gold. Salaries, commodities and everything else available in a normal economy will be priced and paid in Solids, but may be paid in the local currency at the spot exchange rate; same with the payment of taxes. As long as the economy remains relatively stable, both currencies will also keep a stable exchange rate. Should the government of a particular country in the Eurozone decide –due to valid reasons or otherwise– to increase the local currency supply, such a move will most likely be in detriment of its value vis-a-vis the Solid. When the money supply increase is modest, depreciation of the local currency may be mild, and the exchange rate will probably not move dramatically. An excessive money supply increase of the local currency by the local central bank would encourage economic agents to seek refuge in the Solid by demanding payment in said currency instead of the local currency, or in the local currency equivalent at the prevailing exchange rate. As both currencies will have legal tender status, this option should be available.

The possibility of availing governments to increase the money supply will provide an essential feature –lacking in the current Euro system– namely, a "Pressure Valve," but this feature will in turn be tempered by the possibility local economic agents will have to go over to the Solid for all their economic needs, hence limiting the ability of the government to collect the inflation tax. Under a system where economic agents will wield the unequivocal power of "punishing" monetary authorities should they decide to make excessive use of the printing press, such irresistible might will moderate their intentions to do so. We would be hard pressed to think of another more efficient and effective regulating system than this one. Furthermore due to the planned 100 percent gold reserve of the Solid, inflation in terms of the Solid would not be an issue.

The monetary system we propose in not new and a number of similar historical precedents exist, beginning in ancient Greece. Parallel currencies have sometimes had a fixed exchange rate set by law (duo-currencies), while in other cases they competed with each other. We have instances like in China where parallel currencies competed with each other, that is at variable exchange rates– during 200 years of what could be considered a successful monetary system.

Under our DLCCS, member state central banks would deposit whatever amount they wish of their gold holdings in the European Central Bank in exchange for Solids which would be defined as 1/1000th of a gold ounce. Thus, a Solid would be worth ca. US$1.60 at current rates. Total money supply would be the total supply of Solids plus the local currency (drachmas, DMs, FF, Pesetas, etc.) in terms of Solids. The sum of both money supplies would be what we call M_1 narrow money definition. Local currencies will be freely converted in Solids and other local currencies of member states at the spot exchange rate.

In my original DLCCS I had private banks issuing the gold currency as well as state-owned banks, but a good case could be made to leave the issuance of the Solid to the European Central Bank, at least *ab initio*. In any event, it is to be emphasized in the most strongly manner that the DLCCS provides for a gold currency –in this case the Solid - based on the old gold coin standard, with a 100 percent reserve ratio, ensured by law, which was immensely superior to the caricature of such standard enacted under the Bretton Woods agreement. This will of course prevent any arbitrary issuance by the ECB of Solids in excess of 100 percent of the gold holdings as well as money creation from "thin air" as traditionally done by the banking system. Member countries may physically transfer additional amounts of gold to the ECB in exchange for Solid currency, thus increasing their money supply.

The DLCCS' feature which we describe as a "pressure valve" solves the centuries old *conundrum* built into the gold standard, namely, it was abandoned not because it did not work, but because it lacked "flexibility," either real or perceived by politicians who felt hamstrung, and thus it was suspended many times and later diluted before being definitely discarded.

Furthermore, we will argue that given the "pressure valve" mechanism built into the DLCCS there will be no need for any member country to leave the Eurozone on account of the original monetary system rigidity, which will no longer exist. Under the DLCCS countries will keep full sovereignty and governments will be left alone to pursue the monetary policy they deem best, without necessarily affecting other members of the Eurozone.

As a matter of fact, even after the hypothetical exit of countries like Greece, or even Germany, leaving and rendering what some would consider a dangerously mutilated Eurozone, the monetary system we are proposing could be introduced and work as expected all the same, irrespective of who leaves and who stays in the Eurozone.

1 BACKGROUND

The Maastricht Treaty of 1992 created a Eurozone with one currency called the "Euro" which would see the day of light on January 1, 1999 and was adopted by all members, substituting their own local currencies which were then abolished and taken out of circulation. The Euro replaced the "Ecu" which was a European currency unit, based on a basket of currencies. Euro coins and banknotes entered circulation on January 1, 2002. The four main points of the so called Euro Convergence criteria (aka Maastricht Criteria) are based on Article 121[1] of the European Community Treaty and reads as follows:

1. Inflation rates: No more than 1.5 percentage points higher than the average of the three best performing member states of the EU.

2. Government finance:

Annual government deficit: The ratio of the annual government deficit to gross domestic product (GDP) must not exceed 3 percent at the end of the preceding fiscal year. If not it is at least required to reach a level close to 3 percent. Only exceptional and temporary excesses would be granted for exceptional cases.

The ratio of gross government debt to GDP must not exceed 60 percent at the end of the preceding fiscal year. Even if the target cannot be achieved due to the specific conditions, the ratio must have sufficiently diminished and must be approaching the reference value at a satisfactory pace.

3. Exchange rate: Applicant countries should have joined the exchange-rate mechanism (ERM II) under the European Monetary System (EMS) for two consecutive years and should not have devalued its currency during the period.

4. Long-term interest rates: The nominal long-term interest rate must not be more than 2 percentage points higher than in the three lowest inflation member states. The purpose of setting the criteria is to maintain the price stability within the Eurozone even with the inclusion of new member states.

2 A FAILED CONCEPT

"It is nothing less than astonishing to witness the exceptional lack of understanding of essential economic principles exhibited by the Nomenklatura ruling the Eurozone, not only in troubled countries but especially in those who pretend to have solutions to the Eurozone problems."

Eduardo Belgrano

From the moment the Euro was devised and the "Economic Convergence" concept was presented, as *conditio sine qua non* for the new supranational currency to operate as expected, it should have been clear that it was patently absurd and would not work [Belgrano][2]. The essential reason was of course, the fact that circulation of the new single currency would span many political boundaries, and the requirement to uphold economic convergence would subject entirely different economies like Greece and Germany —to name only two— with very different needs with conditions, which some members could simply not meet. They would have to conform to a number of strict economic measures which would, and did, generate not only unwanted economic upheaval but also severe political and social crisis. Recently, five-hundred Greek parents gave up their children because they could not feed them anymore[3]; all in the name of economic convergence. The only way the Euro would work and economic convergence be achieved would be for all Eurozone country members to form a new country along the lines of the old Yugoslavia, a sort of "Europeavia," governed by a "Tito." Not a very plausible scenario occurring any time soon.

It is well known that a community of countries with a regime of fixed exchange rates axiomatically implies a very similar inflation rate level [Claassen][4]

Notwithstanding the obvious differences in the economies of the planned Euro system, politicians as well as many economists acting as

8

enablers, chose to ignore this dictum and the obvious implication, namely, that it would be next to impossible for such dissimilar country members to maintain a long term standardized inflation rate level. Furthermore, that in order to achieve such a utopian objective, countries would necessarily have to relinquish full sovereignty, an exceedingly preposterous proposition. While Europe has come a long way since the times during the first half of the 20th Century in which countries were torn apart due to deep nationalistic feelings, it is highly improbable that any country would agree to relinquish sovereignty.

Recent comments by Jaques Delors[5] one of the architects of the Euro currency, about the reasons why the Euro is failing and the disastrous indebtedness of many of its members, clearly show that he is not able – even today– to grasp the absurdity and the long term unattainability of the "Economic Convergence" concept.

The reality is that the Eurozone is nothing more than an economic zone composed by a "Colonial Power" (Germany) ruling over a number of "colonies" (all the other members). Due to the single currency and other conditions, Germany has been in a position to sell the big bulk of her exports to her "colonies" at prices set in the common currency, neither Germany nor her colonies having to worry about exchange risk. Credit was abundant and paradoxically, we may add that part of the sovereign debt burdening the PIIGS (Portugal, Italy, Ireland, Greece, Spain) countries may have been created precisely to buy German exports.

Every Eurozone country member is under the firm grip of Brussels and the European Central Bank.

The ECB's role includes:

- Setting key interest rates for the Eurozone and controlling the money supply
- Managing the Eurozone's foreign currency reserves and buying or selling currencies when necessary to keep exchange rates in balance
- Helping to ensure financial markets and institutions are adequately supervised by national authorities, and that payment systems function smoothly

- Authorizing central banks in Eurozone countries to issue Euro banknotes
- Monitoring price trends and assessing the risk they pose to price stability.

Source: European Central Bank

In view of the above, countries like Greece, Spain and others were unable to introduce adjustments in their economies, after years of misguided economic policies (not that many sought them). This led to an increase in labor costs, making the country's products more expensive vis-a-vis those of other countries, pricing their products and services out of the market.

The fact was and still is that the Eurozone is composed by countries with very different economies and needs, thus the end results have proved to be catastrophic, which we may add, were expected by anyone who understood the unworkable concept of "Economic Convergence" forced upon members under a supranational environment.

Amazingly, Chancellor Merkel —the unofficial Eurozone *Hegemon*— refuses to come to terms with reality, namely the unequivocal failure of the Euro, and continues to come up with more *Kafkaesque* measures to shore up an unworkable system, the latest being the creation of what Germany called a "fiscal union" to impose "fiscal discipline" on Euro members. In other words, creating more economic misery to most members and striving to take away yet more sovereignty from them.

Furthermore and in addition, it is beyond belief that German political authorities can envision a solution to the problem by imposing additional strict austerity measures on economies which are and have been in recession for a few years, such as Greece. We really do not know at this point if Chancellor Merkel is being disastrously advised by her economics team, or if in reality she is just trying to hold together the Euro system come what may, thus, preserving the coziest business and economic agreement known since Leopold King of the Belgians ruled the Congo as his personal fiefdom.

The possibility of Chancellor Merkel being wretchedly advised by her mainstream economists should not be rejected out of hand. We have had in the past famous economists expounding theories bordering almost on astrology and others expounding very implausible dictums. W. S. Jevons and his "sunspots" theory of economic cycles is a good example of the first kind. Werner Sombart, one of the leading European social scientists during the first quarter of the 20th Century and member of the American Economic Association comes to mind as a good example of the second kind. In one of his books, he explained to us that: "Our *Führer* (Hitler) gets his orders directly from God, the *Führer* of the Universe." He goes on to say that: "We do not know how God communicates with our *Führer*, but the fact cannot be denied."

We cannot tell for sure, but can only hope that whoever is advising Chancellor Merkel in the field of economics doesn't do so based on some arcane economic theory, not even close to the gist of that of W.S. Jevons and his sunspots, nor to one as complex and of such esoteric nature of W. Sombart's insight.

We have then Sig. Mario Draghi, the new president of the European Central Bank in his recent testimony[6] to the European Parliament after being appointed as EBC director stating, "I have no doubt whatsoever about the strength of the Euro, about its permanence, about its irreversibility......" This reminds us of two things, first about Vera Smith's contention[7] that, "Nowadays....... it seems reasonably to suppose that central banks are valued for providing prestigious and comfortable jobs." We could hardly disagree with such a notion. While Smith wrote that statement in 1932, we risk saying that it is still very much current, as these elite bureaucrats try to keep their well-paid jobs by justifying whatever is the *status quo*, whether due to greed or incompetence.

Furthermore, the fact that some EU key personalities such as Jean-Claude Juncker are ready to lie about the economic situation in the Eurozone, and stated so much on the record[8] is not conducive to buttressing confidence in the Eurozone or the Euro.

It would perhaps help towards the perception of solidity of the Euro and the Eurozone survival in general, should Dragi, van Rompuy, Barroso, Juncker and other eminent EU personalities publicly declare their decision to immediately purchase bonds denominated in Euros, issued by the so called PIIGS countries, especially Greece, and have them become a sizeable part of their personal retirement funds.

The other things that reminds us of Sig. Draghi's highfalutin statement that the Euro will not die, is what Prince Otto v. Bismarck said about political news, namely, "Do not believe any political news until it is officially denied." We also tend to agree with such thought.

We must add that on the May 31, 2012 meeting of the European Parliament, Mr Draghi stated that "The Euro is unsustainable without action" which leads us to believe that after uttering the statement about the Euro "strength" (among others) which was likely a thankful note addressed to those who put him in his new job, Mr Draghi must have seen the exceedingly ugly reality, and was, however reluctantly, compelled to publicly acknowledge it.

As most are aware, the banking system in France and especially in Germany are both in a dire situation due to the large holdings of sovereign debt issued by PIIGS countries. In order to create more confidence in European banks, a stress test was performed to find out whether there were any banks in trouble. After the results and the details of the procedure were published, the test was declared a fraud by most analysts. A second stress test was carried out which fared no better in the opinion of observers. The reality is that should one or more of the PIIGS countries default, something which could also be triggered by the demise of the Euro, a few German and French banks could well go into receivership, barring some government bailouts of biblical proportions.

As if the situation in the private banking system of the two biggest economies in the Eurozone wouldn't be enough trouble, a report about certain investments of the German Bundesbank was recently published[9] compounding the problem. This report reveals that the Bundesbank has lent the European Central Bank through the so- called Target2 –the ECB interbank payments system– almost half a trillion Euros against a collateral composed of sovereign debt issued by all the troubled countries in the Eurozone. To find information about these loans classified as "claims" it is necessary to dig deeply into the footnotes of the reports of central banks of the seventeen country members of the Eurozone. In the event of a demise of the Eurozone, the Bundesbank could lose this gigantic amount of money. This may help explain the desperation exhibited by Chancellor Merkel in her quest for a solution to maintain the current status quo, no matter what the cost or how absurd it may be.

3 THE GOLD STANDARD

*"Gold is not necessary. I have no interest in gold.
We will build a solid state, without an ounce of
gold behind it. Anyone who sells above the set
prices, let him be marched off to a concentration
camp. That's the bastion of money."*
Adolf Hitler

*"In the absence of the gold standard, there is no
way to protect savings from confiscation through
inflation...."*
Alan Greenspan

The gold standard has been –in various forms– either *de jure* or *de facto* part of the monetary system of many countries at one time or another for the past few thousand years. However it has been maligned by many, the evidence shows that it brought, or to be more accurate forced monetary discipline upon politicians, limiting their discretionary capacity to issue paper money and spend. One fallacy very commonly encountered which denigrates the quality and benefits of operating under the gold standard is that "it was not perfect," without saying so much. While it is certainly not perfect, it is difficult not to realize its superiority vis-a-vis *fiat* standards which have enabled politicians and why not say it, many economists the implementation and recommendation of all kinds of economic and political follies.

Critiques to the benefits of operating under the gold standard come in many forms; some are difficult to understand though. Phillip Cagan writes in one paper[10] that "the gold standard was not viewed as adequate to provide the desired behavior of prices." He wrote further that during the gold standard era in the United States between 1897 and

1914 wholesale prices rose 40 percent. While wholesale prices differ from the CPI in a few ways, we are at a loss to understand how an average yearly 2 percent compounded increase can be considered or implied to be such a great failure of the gold standard to prevent inflation. We should also emphasize that Cagan selected a specific short period of time which could be countered by the results of Professor Roy W. Jastram[11] who summarizes his findings on the subject as follows:

"From 1792 into the 1930s Britain was on the gold standard and the U.S. was either on a bimetallic standard or one of gold alone. During all those years, in both countries price inflations and subsequent deflations average sensibly to zero. The result: For both the U.K. and the U.S. the wholesale price index numbers at the end of the gold standard were at just the level of 1800"

In the same essay however, Mr. Cagan makes another observation, this one we believe, with merit. Discussing the lack of benefits that convertibility under a gold standard brought over monetary policy, he argues [Cagan]^(op. cit. P.24), and we quote: "The gold standard symbolizes a commitment to price stability. It provides neither the commitment nor the procedure to achieve it, which, must be found elsewhere. If a nation can make the commitment, it does not need the gold standard. Without the commitment, a standard is irrelevant."

It is also to be emphasized that the gold standard can strictly operate as expected when four conditions are met [Williams][12] : 1) when there are no surplus gold reserves in the banking system and a loss of gold must mean a shrinkage of bank credit; 2) when there are no international capital movements so that, on balance, exports of goods must equal imports and any excess over the other must induce a corrective flow of gold; 3) when unit cost of production are responsive to the movement of prices; 4) when international demand responds freely to changes in prices, so that a fall of prices will produce an increase in value of exports relative to imports, and contrariwise. Given these conditions, trade changes are corrected by the interaction of gold flows and prices. A fulfillment of these four conditions occurred rarely and when it did, during short periods of time. As a matter of fact, the Bank of England, for instance, had its discount rate policy designed to protect its gold reserves. By increasing the bank rate it would discourage

British foreign lending, attract funds and stop the gold outflow [Williams][op.cit].

As a matter of fact, "gold points" (the limits of the market exchange rates bands which signaled when it became profitable to ship gold between countries) were quite often violated. In his study of gold point violations between 1890 and 1914, Clark[13] tells us that said violations were persistent, that gold flowed in apparently unprofitable directions and of the intervention of monetary authorities in England and the U.S. thwarting the correct operation of the gold standard system. This seems to lend support to Cagan's assertion cited above, concerning the irrelevance of re-introducing the gold standard as a means to assure monetary discipline.

While the gold standard system provided clear rules, these were very often not followed. Banks were not allowed their reserve ratios to go below their legal limits. Banks suspending convertibility of their notes would be declared insolvent. However, in the U.S. this was not only quite common, but also government sanctioned [Smith[(op.cit.)]. On many occasions the Comptroller of the Currency allowed banks to suspend convertibility for many months, and then allowed them to resume business on the condition that their assets should be "sound." This happened on occasions in which the bank in question was in bankruptcy.

The purpose of this section dealing with the gold standard is in no way intended to be an exposition of why the gold standard is an inadequate, even outdated, monetary system. The reality is that the gold standard was the best monetary system that ever was, serving humanity well for thousands of years. We merely attempted to point out that, because it was too good, it was tampered with to allow politicians to maintain a certain "discretionary capacity" in the setting of monetary policies to suit their objectives. While it was certainly not perfect and many would want to justify its inadequacy by such a notion, it is difficult not to agree with Cagan and many others in the sense that tampering with the gold standard to enable a good measure of discretionary monetary policy, is not much different to government policies under a *fiat* currency system, which were and are routinely bent and even broken to attain the same objective. In short, very regretfully, we must conclude that the gold standard monetary system carries the seeds of its own destruction.

4 THE OPTIMAL CURRENCY AREAS THEORY

"Maybe it isn't possible to create a European
government that is modeled after an existing
government….. "But it will be achieved because,
for Europe, it isn't just the best game in town, it's
the only game."
Robert Mundell

In 1961 Robert Mundell wrote a seminal paper[14] dealing with the *conundrum* confronted by countries with different economic fundamentals to introduce economic correcting measures to help one area without affecting another. Mundell writes[15]:

"In a currency area comprising different countries with national currencies, the pace of unemployment in deficit countries is set by the willingness of surplus countries to inflate. But in a currency area comprising many regions and a single currency, the pace of inflation is set by the willingness of central authorities to allow unemployment in deficit regions"

This sums up well enough the current predicament of Brussels as the central authority enforcing economic convergence, which is forced upon some Eurozone members, creating unemployment and various social and economic suffering. All this for the sake of avoiding inflation in those countries with low unemployment.

The Ricardian assumption concerning labor mobility, if true at an international level would alleviate the imbalances of unemployment and inflation. Regretfully, this labor mobility concept is in essence a myth; it simply does not occur in any significant magnitude as to solve the inter-country imbalances. The reasons for this are many, one being that the skills required in one country may be different than those possessed by people willing to relocate; language barriers and habits are others. Perfect mobility within two countries, for example, would of course go a long way in achieving currency integration. Those two countries could conceivably form an optimal currency area and peg their currencies one to the other [Kenen][16]

Europe is certainly not an exception when citing the problems of introducing one single supranational currency unit in a region comprised of many countries [Kafka][17]

To visually fathom the problematic impact of economic convergence, the U.S. map below has the states renamed for countries with roughly similar GDPs[18]. The point of the map is to envision how some very different economies with different economic needs and social objectives could work under the economic convergence concept, that is, it could only be achieved under one country and one government with central authority. We can see *prima facie* that this would be a monumental task to be achieved by one currency, in this case, the Dollar. Now, suppose that each "state" depicted on the map would have independent governments, and the absurdity of the Euro and economic convergence become rather evident.

5 HISTORICAL PRECEDENTS OF CURRENCY COMPETITION

"The history of government management of money has, except for a few short happy periods, been one of incessant fraud and deception."
Friedrich August von Hayek

Contrary to some opinions [Engels][19] cases of parallel currencies —either national or foreign currencies— circulating side-by-side competing with each other in history have been abundant and in some cases have lasted for centuries. This should not be confused with cases of "dollarization" for example, where the U.S. currency circulates within a country together with the local currency. A situation such as the one described above has been occurring in some countries for decades now and still occurs, as for example in Uruguay. The local currency is the Uruguayan peso, but everyone talks about U.S. dollars when referring to salaries, real estate and everything else, and the American currency actually circulates physically and is accepted across the board. The difference with our DLCCS is that the overwhelming majority of Uruguayans do not earn salaries denominated in dollars, nor they pay their taxes in the American currency. Due to this, the ability of the government to collect the inflation tax remains almost intact and the dollar can be considered more of a unit of account than a legitimate parallel currency.

The first known parallel currency is the gold stater [Vaubel][20] which in the 7th Century BC circulated side-by-side with various silver coins at a flexible exchange rate. There were many other examples, allegedly in ancient Egypt and Rome, as well as during the Merovingian and Carolingian dynasties [Vaubel][op.cit.]. Between the 16th and 18th centuries the silver Thaler, the gold Ducat and gold Guilder circulated side-by-side at variable exchange rates [Vaubel][op.cit.]. While there were reference exchange rates for the various circulating coins of gold and silver, the

Reichsmünzordnung of 1559, which for two centuries formed the basis of the German currency system, stated clearly that the official rates between circulating coins should not be considered as a legal or forced rate. [Vaubel][op.cit.].

There were further examples of parallel currency systems in other countries. We will now turn to the Chinese experience with gold and silver currencies competing with each other.

Between 1650 and 1850 China was under a monetary system where copper coins ("cash") and silver bullion ("taels") circulated side-by-side as monetary units, at flexible exchange rates [Chen][21]. While the government tried to set a fixed exchange rate between copper cash and silver bullion, this was not possible due to the imperfect substitutability of the two types of currencies. Hence, instead of succeeding in maintaining bimetallism, the reality is that China was under a monetary system of two-metallic currencies circulating at variable exchange rates. A dual price regime emerged where some items were priced in copper cash while others were in silver bullion.

Copper cash was more often used for small transactions (such as agricultural products) while silver was preferred to transact more valuable commodities. Due to the dual price structure, whenever the fundamental of key commodities changed, the exchange rate of the currencies also changed in response to it.

Silver taels were mostly cast by silversmiths while copper coins were minted by the government; there was also a considerable counterfeiting activity of copper coins circulating side-by-side with the real ones. There were also foreign silver coins circulating such as U.S. dollars.

At times, shortage of copper developed which caused many copper cash coins to be melted to cast utensils, as well as to make smaller coins. It could be argued that the supply of copper coins was determined by the public.

While there were complaints that the complexity of the system benefitted banks and money changers greatly, one has to wonder how was it possible that it persisted for so long. Professor Chau Nan

Chen[op.cit.] explains that the reason has to do with the theory of Optimal Currency Areas, namely, that when mobility of labor between regions is low or nonexistent (land being an important factor of production is immobile par excellence), then the regions should have different currencies.

During 1800-1850 China experienced important an influx of silver and a shortage of copper which altered the exchange rate in favor of copper cash coins. This trend was reversed when China's favorable balance of trade suffered due to increasing imports of opium and the ensuing outflow of silver.. Some data is available for two towns located far apart and used to elaborate a consumer price index or cost of living of sorts. Results show that while the price of commodities hovered around a given price, the purchase power of silver nearly doubled during the period of interest. The reason for this is attributed to the outflow of silver due to opium imports and the debasement of copper coins and the latter most likely occurred to mitigate the effects of the deflationary pressures caused by a shortage of monetary silver..

This above described situation affected not only business and banks but also the collection of taxes from the part of the government which was denominated in silver and could only be paid in copper cash, but at an exchange rate much higher than the market. Salt, a government monopoly, also had to be paid for in silver. On the other hand, peasants and salt merchants received copper cash when doing business. As expected, government income due to salt sales and tax collection dropped to an alarming level. It also created confrontations between landlords and tenants due to the fact that leases were quoted in silver. The same thing happened between manufacturers and workers who received payment of their salaries in copper cash.

The outflow of silver had a deflationary effect on the economy, a redistribution of income within the private sector as well between the government and the private sector. The negative effect would have been even greater had China been on a silver only monetary standard. Furthermore, the fiscal problems were created by the inflexible policy of accepting silver only in payment of taxes. The government could have mitigated the problem, had it issued paper currency backed by copper coin. The government, however, was opposed to doing this to avoid an out-of-control situation, just as in the past when paper money was over issued.

6 THE DLCCS-DUAL LEVEL CURRENCY COMPETITION SYSTEM

"The past instability of the market economy is the consequence of the exclusion of the most important regulator of the market mechanism, money, from itself being regulated by the market process."
Friedrich August v. Hayek

The original name for the new gold currency we offered in the various articles we wrote on the subject beginning in the 1980s was the "Real" [Belgrano][22], which was subsequently appropriated (copied?) by Brazil when it introduced a new currency with said name in 1994. For the sake of causing the least possible confusion, we will then call the new gold supranational currency "Solid" which is derived from the Roman/Byzantine "Solidus" a gold coin (struck in small quantities by Diocletian and minted once more by Constantine in 312 AD) which due to its purity was highly sought after and readily accepted within the known world. As a small digression, we would argue that the reason for the Byzantine Empire lasting ca. 1100 years was due to its excellent monetary system based on the gold Solidus, as well as to the monopoly of the so-called "Greek Fire," a weapon which could arguably be called the atomic bomb of antiquity.

The Solid will be issued with 100 percent gold reserve, in view of which the fractional reserve banking will not operate. The core procedure involved in fractional reserve banking would be a fraudulent operation should a private person engage in it.

Definition of 'Fractional Reserve Banking' according to *Investopedia*: "A banking system in which only a fraction of bank deposits are backed by actual cash-on-hand and are available for withdrawal. This is done to expand the economy by freeing up capital that can be loaned out to other parties. Most countries operate under this type of system."

Investopedia further explains 'Fractional Reserve Banking'

"Many U.S. banks were forced to shut down during the Great Depression because so many people attempted to withdraw assets at the same time. Today there are many safeguards in place to prevent such an instance from occurring again, but the fractional-reserve banking system remains in place."

Because 100 percent of the gold represented by the Solid must be physically deposited at the banks, the perils involved in the fractional reserve banking system will not apply.

The whole economy will be expressed in Solid terms —private as well as public companies and institutions— including salaries, transfer payments, contracts, securities, taxes, international commerce and more. Anyone will be able to use the local currency to pay for anything quoted in Solids at the prevailing spot exchange rate.

An options and forward market for the local currency/Solid exchange will likely develop to cater for the needs of businessmen and producers among others.

Also, the DLCCS envisions competition between all the *fiat* currencies vis-a-vis the gold currency, as well as competition among the private issuers of the latter (once they are allowed to issue Solids). Private issuers will derive *seigniorage* defined as the difference between the cost of buying gold, warehousing it and printing the notes vis-a-vis the price in which the notes are sold in exchange either for gold or other currencies at the spot exchange rate. Many gold investors will rather hold "Solid" notes which are convertible into gold than the physical gold which cannot be invested at interest, plus the fact that it costs money to warehouse. To help the swift adoption of the new currency, we will *ab initio* designate the European Central Bank as the only authorized issuer of the Solid.

In any event there will be competition not only between *fiat* currencies and the Solid but also among *fiat* currencies themselves which will be exchanged at variable exchange rates.

The lack of flexibility of the gold standard (to allow discretionary monetary policy) which hamstrung politicians was the cause of its demise. Our DLCCS allows this flexibility without destroying the system, while at the same time providing for a self-regulating mechanism implemented by human action. It is based on what we denominate the "Theory of the Pressure Valve" which postulates that "A monetary system either based on commodities or economic policies will succeed and survive in its original conceptualization, only if there is a measure of flexibility built into this system, coupled with a self regulating feature designed to uphold said original conceptualization."

It is also necessary to be mentioned that, while it would seem to be true that most discretionary spending carried out by politicians has to do with misguided reasons, there are –in our judgment– instances in which money expansion is up to a certain extent justified, especially in case of catastrophic events such as those from natural causes. Bolivia during the administration of Hernan Siles Suazo is a good example[23]. In cases as the latter, monetary expansion by the government is urgently required to pay for resources. Regretfully, amounts of money created *ab-nihilo* in response to catastrophic situations have however invariably ended up in creating inflationary, sometimes hyperinflationary economies. Hyperinflation did occur in Bolivia as a consequence of Siles Suazo's monetary expansion.

Central banks of country members may also purchase gold (using local currency as well as their foreign currency holdings) and transfer it to the ECB in order to increase their Solids supply. Should that country decide to print excessive amounts of the local currency to purchase gold, it will have to pay more of it each time to buy the precious metal. Hence, such a strategy will end up being a futile, self-defeating exercise, generating loss of confidence in the local currency and accelerating its depreciation constraining the capacity of the government to influence the economy by means of the management of the local currency.

Monetary confidence is vital for any country's interests, and even its survival; for example, the production of national defense. Benjamin Klein[24] writes on the subject:

"Control of the country's dominant money supply carries with it the ability to quickly gain control of a significant quantity of the country's resources. To a government such control represents a very large potential tax that can quickly be levied and collected in a broad way and efficient way – without market or democratic tests. If the government holds it coercion capital in such a highly liquid form the asset can then be conveniently used for national defense purposes. England, for example exhausted a large part of the pound sterling brand name capital, built up over more than two centuries of successful performance, to fight World War II."

Monetary authorities may increase the local money supply to "help" with a particular problem and quickly "sterilize" it (withdraw from circulation) to prevent any major adverse movement in the Solid/local currency exchange rate.

People would hardly be put off should prices be quoted in Solids as well as in the local currency. The latest example being the local European currencies and the Euro, during the phasing out period between 1998 and 2002 in which merchandise was quoted in the local currency as well as in Euros.

The money supply in each country will be composed of Solids and the local currency, and to arrive at the total money supply (M_T) it will be necessary to add up the money supply in Solids (M_S) plus the money supply expressed in the local currency (M_{LC}) converted at the prevailing exchange rate. However, it is to be strongly emphasized that the money supply expressed in Solidus will be defined as the total amount of physical notes and coin circulating in the economy plus notes and coin held at private banks and the European Central Bank. The money supply represented by the local currency (M_{LC}) on the other hand will suit the definition of M_1 which essentially includes currency in the economy plus demand deposits.

The Solid will be a currency with a 100 percent gold backing and therefore cannot be arbitrarily created *ex-nihilo* as is the case with *fiat* currencies, thus mostly escaping the control of politicians and Central Bank elite bureaucrats. As a matter of fact, after the DLCCS is introduced, the payroll of the European Central Bank should probably be halved, not a popular measure especially among those earning lavish salaries and generous fringe benefits, but a reasonable one based on the necessary work to be carried out.

Inflation as measured by the CPI in Solid terms will tend toward zero [Belgrano][25]. While local currencies may depreciate in terms of the Solid, M_T definition of money supply will be expressed in Solid terms. This means that in the event of money expansion of the local currency, prices may increase in terms of the local currency, however the latter will depreciate vis-a-vis the Solid. Hence, increase of prices in terms of Solids will hardly occur in any significant magnitude, therefore the concept of "money illusion" referred to savings and income will not apply. Furthermore, the alleged trade-off between unemployment and inflation depicted by the Phillips Curve (disproved by stagflation episodes in the 1970s) could not operate under the DLCCS due to the built-in "pressure valve" mechanism.

Inflation in terms of Solids on the other hand could conceivably occur provided exceedingly huge amounts of gold are suddenly available to issue the corresponding amount of Solids. We do envision gold especially from private hoards —small and large— being brought to the ECB to exchange it for Solids which would likely enter in circulation as investment capital. Furthermore, we do not reject out of hand the possibility that even foreign holders of large gold hoards, including central banks, may decide to deposit their precious metal holdings with the ECB exchanging it for Solids. The ECB can of course decide when and how much of the gold available will be used as backing to issue Solids and such a policy should further help prevent inflation in terms of Solids.

It is well known that gold is at times an attractive investment when people expect an increase in its value. The well known drawback of investing in gold on the other hand is that it does not earn interest. The fact that the Solid will be a currency unit backed 100 percent by gold, which can be invested and earn interest with no warehousing costs, should make it a very attractive alternative to the purchase of gold bullion.

There are no reliable estimates of private gold holdings, but there is no doubt that world individual and institutional (private) gold holdings run in the thousands of metric tons, especially in countries like India. We do not know to what extent these private holdings would play a role in the Solid money supply.

It would be a healthy, advisable measure (but not absolutely necessary; really more of a rhetorical nature) to limit or outright disallow the issuance of sovereign debt expressed in Solids by all member countries. Otherwise, in a way this would be a sort of back door for politicians to increase Ms, without having "earned" the amounts in Solids; for example by means of the country achieving a positive balance of trade and/or a net investment in the balance of payments. Instead government will be free to issue paper denominated in the local currencies or in dollars, pounds and other foreign currencies, and if they wish buy gold to issue in turn Solids. The difference is that by using this procedure akin to the printing press approach governments would have to pay increasingly higher rates of interest to finance their purchases of Solids, adding to M_S thus increasing M_T. The monetization of debt in terms of Solids will be a more difficult affair for the government, due to the 100 percent gold reserve. Under a DLCCS government issue of bonds cannot be paid by the Central Bank simply by increasing banks' monetary base unless the Solids are available.

A significant gold inflation, such as it occurred in the 1500s in Europe, would require the sudden discovery of gold above ground and mining deposits equivalent to what Cortes and Pizarro found in Mexico and Peru, respectively, plus a substantial increase in the European production of precious metals (especially silver) as it occurred predating the influx of precious metals from Latin America into Europe. Such a scenario is not very realistic.

Some may argue that transaction costs would be higher when more than one currency is in circulation [Guggenheim][26], as it would be the case under the DLCCS, as opposed to a single currency monetary system. While this may well be true, it will simply be the cost of having a functional, long term effective, stable monetary system without inflation and most of all, a system which would bring discretionary spending –and all the maladies associated with it– under control. Just as buying and installing a lock is the cost of securing a door, preventing the entrance of undesirable people.

7 CONVERTING THE EURO MONETARY SYSTEM INTO A DLCCS

> *"Greece has given Europe the opportunity to fix a defect in the Eurozone, that is the fact that we did not have a fiscal union. Now steps have been taken to begin that process. And there is more solidarity from nation to nation, and that is a good thing. That has been Greece's gift to Europe."*
>
> Georgios A. Papandreou

At the present time, adding up all the gold reserves holdings at the Eurozone member central banks and the total amount of Euros issued, it is estimated that there is ca. 5 percent gold backing in round numbers. This may vary but it is irrelevant to the functioning of the system; the real amount will be factored in when the time comes.

We will define the Solid as 1000th of a troy ounce of gold. There will be denominations of 1,000, 500, 100, 50, 10 and 5 solid notes. Coins will also be issued in the traditional denominations, including $1.00.

Each Euro would be worth in gold 5 percent in terms of the Solid which further means that € 1,000 equals $50 Solids or that $1.00 = € 20.00. Hence, each Solid (S) will be issued in exchange for 20 Euros.

NOTES:
- Due to the definition of the Solid (1000th of a gold ounce) and the price of gold the conversion ratio can be different; we use 1/20 for simplicity reasons. It is irrelevant if values change as when the moment comes they can be re-adjusted as required.

- It is also a fact that central banks in each member country have different amounts of gold holdings, and thus the amount of Solids they will get from the ECB will be different. This however is not important, as the difference in money supply will be covered by the issuance of the local currency in a sufficient amount.

For all practical purposes what the above means is that the money supply in the Eurozone in terms of Euros will contract by 95 percent that is, it will suddenly shrink to 5 percent of its previous supply. Under normal circumstances this huge money supply contraction would likely cause a catastrophic economic recession/depression. Here is where the benefit of the DLCCS shines in its practicality, as each Eurozone member will then issue an amount in local currency to be determined which could conceivable be of such a magnitude as to make up for the 95 percent money supply shortfall at the original rate in which legacy currencies were exchanged by Euros. Now a country like Greece for example will have *ex post facto* the same nominal money supply made up of Solids and Drachmas as the economy had *ex ante* in terms of Euros.

As explained by Chau Nan Chen[op.cit.] describing the Chinese experience with parallel currencies, the deflation caused by the outflow of silver was made severe due to misguided government measures and would have been much worse, had copper not circulated side-by-side with silver. The functioning of the DLCCS would be devoid of the hurdles encountered in China as described in the Chinese parallel currency episode, and will operate in a much smoother way.

No private or public debt, bank accounts nor contracts will suffer any disturbance except the currency adjustment (20 to 1) plus receive the additional money in local currency to make up for the 95 percent Euro holding. The rate at which for example, Drachmas were exchanged for Euros in 2002 was 341 (340.75) drachmas in round numbers for one Euro. The following table illustrates the exchange rate of all legacy currencies vis-a-vis de Euro in 2002.

Conversion Table For Legacy to Euro Currency

Country	Currency	Foreign Amount	/	Conversion Rate	Euro Amount
Austria	Austria Schilling	ATS	Divided by	13.760300	= 1 EUR
Belgium	Belgian Franc	BEF	Divided by	40.339900	= 1 EUR
Germany	Deutsche Mark	DEM	Divided by	1.955830	= 1 EUR
Spain	Spanish Peseta	ESP	Divided by	166.386000	= 1 EUR
Finland	Finnish Markka	FIM	Divided by	5.945730	= 1 EUR
France	French Franc	FRF	Divided by	6.559570	= 1 EUR
Greece	Greek Drachma	GRD	Divided by	340.750000	= 1 EUR
Ireland	Irish Pound	IEP	Divided by	.787564	= 1 EUR
Italy	Italian Lira	ITL	Divided by	1936.270000	= 1 EUR
Luxemburg	Luxembourg Franc	LUF	Divided by	40.339900	= 1 EUR
The Netherlands	Dutch Guilder	NLG	Divided by	2.203710	= 1 EUR
Portugal	Portuguese Escudo	PTE	Divided by	200.482000	= 1 EUR

Under the DLCCS, the formula to calculate the amount of currency each economic agent will receive in exchange for Solids is:

Solids $= €/20$

Local currency delivered to make up the shortfall $= (€- S)*LR$

Where € is Euros, 20 represents the amount of Euros for one Solid, S is solid and LR represents the original exchange rate between the legacy currencies and the Euro valid in 2002. This equivalence may have certainly changed but we shall use it for the purpose of our argument. In any event, it is of course possible to determine an exchange rate deemed more accurate when the moment comes.

Checking, savings and all type of accounts in Euros will be converted to Solids and credited with the corresponding additional amounts of local currency. For example, say a person has €20,000 in a savings account at the National Bank of Greece. This client will receive currency as follows:

| Amount in Solids | = 20,000/20 | = 1,000 Solids |
| Amount in Drachmas | = (20,000-1,000)*341 | = 6,479,000 Drachmas |

This account will exhibit a credit of $1,000 plus 6,479,000 drachmas; Euros will be withdrawn from circulation. Contracts and bonds worth €20,000 –continuing with the same example– will be now worth $1,000 plus 6,479,000 Drachmas. An individual earning a monthly salary of say, €4,200, will now receive $210 plus 1,360,590 Drachmas.

The conversion and exchange of Euros for Solids and Drachmas will take place in a manner not unlike that which was carried out when legacy currencies were converted and exchanged into Euros in 2002.

Deposits belonging to Greek citizens in banks in other member countries, for example, will be credited with the 20 to 1 conversion in said country plus the additional credit in the newly reissued local currency (Deutsche Marks, Pesetas, Schillings, etc.).

While it is possible that at the beginning the Drachma and other weak currencies will lose value vis-a-vis the Solid, after some months it is expected that they will stabilize. Additionally, the holdings in Solids will increase in purchasing power.

It is conceivable that Euro holders in the so-called PIIGS countries (Portugal, Italy, Ireland, Greece, Spain) will look to open accounts in Euros in countries like Germany and France to "benefit" by having their deposits converted into Solids and German Marks and French Francs, instead of say, Solids and Escudos or Solids and Drachmas. However, banks in every EU member country may freeze for a certain period of time the opening of accounts by non-residents once the conversion mechanism is published.

The mechanism described above is one way in which countries can inject liquidity into the economy in a very direct and swift way to make up for the money supply shrinkage brought about by the introduction of the Solid.

The situation will then theoretically be that each country will start out with the same money supply as the *ex ante* economy had before expressed in Euros, without economic agents suffering any loss due to the introduction of the DLCCS. It is very likely that Greeks, for example, will attempt to increase their Solids holdings by buying Solids and paying with their drachmas, which may cause some short term depreciation of the Drachma. We have seen this occurring especially in Latin American countries where depreciation of the local currencies sharply increases demand for the U.S. dollar. However, people need to continue covering their short-term expenses and living needs in general which causes them to begin exchanging their Dollar holdings back into the local currencies, not long after they bought the Dollars halting the depreciation rate of the local currency.

Education of the economic agents about the new monetary system and what they can expect will also play a role.

At the beginning, Gresham's Law (bad money drives out good money from circulation) may take effect, especially in the PIIGS countries where people will hoard Solids and use the local currency to pay for services and products. However, for reasons already explained, we believe this will be a relatively short-lived situation.

Greece –as well as other highly indebted Eurozone country members– will now have to strike a balance between growth and the need to introduce austerity measures through an economic policy designed by Greeks and not imposed by Brussels (read Germany). The other significant benefit of the DLCCS is that under such system a Greek-designed economic policy will not affect either Germany, France or any other Eurozone member. Furthermore, at least citizens in these two countries may relish the idea of having Deutsche Marks and Francs again as their national currencies.

During autumn 1923 in Germany, 1783 printing presses worked day and night for the government to produce the rapidly depreciating *Reichmark*. The paper to print them was in turn produced by 30 paper mills involving 30,000 workers. Additionally, because even these enormous amounts did not cover the demand, more than 5,800 cities, companies and associations issued their own private currencies (*Notgeldscheine*). This (and other hyperinflationary episodes) should be a clear warning to any of the weak Eurozone members not to issue local

35

currency in an excessive manner, under the DLCCS. It will certainly not be necessary to reach the money expansion levels attained during the Weimar Republic in order for its citizens to imitate their 1920s German counterparts in their *Flucht in die Sachwerte*, to protect their savings and wealth by converting their local currency holdings into Solids.

One interesting fact –but not too surprising– is that at the height of the German hyperinflation, all the currency in circulation could have been redeemed in gold by the *Reichsbank* at a much lower ratio than before the war [Helfferich][27], that is, more money for less gold.

Once the Solid conversion becomes a *fait accompli* we anticipate private people bringing their gold to private banks to exchange it for Solids and invest the proceeds at interest; thus savings will increase, investment will be more available and growth will be made possible. This will increase the total money supply in real terms that is, expressed in Solids. By then private banks may either have an agreement with the European Central Bank, or be allowed to issue their own 100 percent gold-backed Solids. Private people may also buy gold with their local currency at the spot price.

We also envision the Solid becoming the preferred currency within other regions outside the Eurozone, *in lieu* of the U.S. dollar.

Continuing with the example of Greece and due to the current dire economic situation, in order to move forward she will probably expand the money supply denominated in drachmas which will cause a devaluation vis-a-vis the Solid. It will be up to her to follow a responsible monetary policy by limiting the Drachma money supply expansion, trying to sterilize it (withdraw the excess from circulation) as soon as possible. Should Greece choose to expand the Drachma money supply in an irresponsible fashion, the subsequent devaluation of the drachma will lead to a diminished capacity to collect the inflation tax from the part of the government and an increase in the level of inflation. It will be up to the Greeks to remediate the situation by voting the administration out of office, with neither political intervention nor economic pressure from Brussels to bear upon them.

It is to be emphasized that by adopting the DLCCS there will be no need for any country (PIIGS or not) to leave the Eurozone in order to get rid of the obligations and limitations imposed by the Euro. As a matter of fact, a *quasi* DLCCS could conceivably be introduced in selected countries only. For example, it could be introduced in Greece only, where the Solid would circulate with the Drachma while all the other Eurozone country members will continue to use the Euro as their sole currency.

This would be a faulty, partial solution, as the Euro would continue to be a currency controlled by politicians and subject to their whims, and would lack the solidity of the proposed DLCCS as well as its long-term solution nature.

.

8 SOVEREIGN DEBT

"Is sovereign debt the new subprime?"
Title of an article on yahoo Finance

There are only two ways of approaching this issue, namely, either the debtor country pays or does not pay its debts. In the event of a default or *quasi* default, the country in question would have to negotiate the terms of default with its creditors. Such possible negotiations are beyond the scope of this essay. A country wishing to pay its debt on the other hand, will have to have the means to do it, something that nowadays politicians in Germany seem not to understand when imposing draconian austerity measures on highly indebted countries that are members of the Eurozone. These measures will prevent any growth of their GDP, thus making it next to impossible to fulfill their financial obligations vis-a-vis their creditors.

The peculiar aspect of all this is the fact that by accepting the strict austerity policies essentially being promoted by German politicians and for reasons explained above, it is a way of "shooting yourself on the foot". Not only private banks but also the Bundesbank has a great, very unhealthy exposure to the so called PIIGS countries. Any of these economically weak countries leaving the Euro system will probably do so under a framework of national bankruptcy which would have untold ripple effects on other countries, including of course, Germany.

9 LEGAL QUESTIONS

"Should a substandard solution to the euro
muddle be introduced, where debtors are forced to
pay their debts in Euros while working in a local
currency environment, social upheaval may ensue
with unfathomable consequences"
Eduardo Belgrano

One very important issue troubling politicians from countries envisioning a hypothetical exit from the Eurozone is the legal aspect of impacting people who will earn salaries in the newly reissued local currency and at the same time hold debts in Euros. For obvious reasons, this matter worries also politicians in those countries where there are many companies holding these notes as creditors. This should not be a problem under the DLCCS.

The Euro will become the Solid which means that all private and government debts will be redeemed in Solids at the rate of 20 Euro to one Solid plus the corresponding local currency amount. Hence, even citizens of countries no longer members of the Eurozone will be able to collect debts in Solids as well as be obliged to pay debts in the same currency. All accounts will be adjusted to reflect the value of the new currency. Thus people who have €20,000 deposited in say, Deutsche Bank, Hellenic Bank or Banco de Santander for example, will have their checking accounts reflecting now a value of $1,000 plus DM 37,240, $1,000 plus Drachmas 6,479,000 and $1,000 plus Pts 3,154,000 respectively.

The Solid will be convertible into gold on demand; minimum amount accepted for conversion will be 100 ounces or $100,000. This can be modified once the status quo becomes accepted.

The same will occur with government issued debt– that is, bonds and bills of any kind.

10 STOCHASTIC SIMULATION TESTING

"Stochastic models represent the real world, while deterministic models are based on arbitrary static, single point data which may make models more tractable but much less realistic"
Eduardo Belgrano

There is an old joke about economists that goes like this: There were these three professors, a physicist, an engineer and a mainstream economist, stranded in an uninhabited island. They only had one sealed can of beans but nothing to open it with. The engineer said, let's get a rock and hit it until it opens. The physicist said it would be better if they put it under the sun until it bursts open. They both asked the economist whether he had a better idea…he responded in the affirmative saying "First, let's assume we have a can opener…"

However ludicrous, this is mainly the way in which mainstream economists build their economic models.

We will model the DLCCS using stochastic simulation which essentially involves departing from probability distributions defining the data, *in lieu* of single point values as is traditional in deterministic models. Any forecast based on deterministic empirical data is apt to suffer from the vagaries of the ever-changing needs, whims and desires of people and their decisions, thus affecting the forecast. It is not possible to model the human mind by applying deterministic processes, something which too many economists refuse to come to terms with. The "let's assume" premise is hardly a solid stepping stone upon which to build credible forecasts and models, and the *ceteris paribus* dictum has been richly abused for too long; the reality is that hardy anything remains equal. Working in the real world one must provide for the fact that changes in consumer preferences and the occurrence of endogenous and exogenous shocks (random events) undercut any pretense of *ceteris paribus* constraints.

We are all very much accustomed to reading about forecasts and models built by economists, based on assumptions which many times (too many times, actually) do not hold: Economics is a social science dealing with people and thus is more of a living organism than an engine which can be built on premises defined by natural sciences like physics and mathematics. When rocket scientists build a missile that goes off course missing the target, it is possible for those scientists to review the architecture of the missile, correct whatever mistake, re-launch it and hit the intended target. In the case of economics, there is hardly right or wrong; only economic agents changing their minds.

The rationale of government intervention is based precisely on the premise that somehow the right information is magically available. While it is of course a *Fata Morgana*, this premise makes the problem more "tractable" and is thus blithely abused.

At the same time that stating it is rather difficult to model the human mind, we should also mention that even natural sciences can sometimes have serious trouble in reaching certainty though a deterministic approach. A good example in quantum mechanics (aka quantum physics) is depicted by the Heisenberg principle which postulates that certain pairs of variables do not "commute." They cannot be brought into precise focus simultaneously. In other words, it is impossible to simultaneously measure the present position while also determining the future motion of a particle or of any system small enough to require quantum mechanical treatment; it calls for a probabilistic approach to deal with it.

Nobel prize-winner physicist Murray Gell-Mann once said, "Imagine how hard physics would be if particles could think." Well, these particles (economic agents) do think and change their minds often which should make it clear how hopeless it is to build models based on arbitrary "assumption", just to make the model "tractable" however detached from the real world.

We could argue that change is the only constant in an economic environment. We will now postulate that economic scenarios are the outcome brought about by three vectors impinging on and interacting within a non spatial continuum. These three vectors are: 1) the economic status quo; 2) the decisions economic agents make vis-a-vis the economic status quo; 3) random events.

Our very simple simulation model using the Montecarlo Method factors in the three vectors included in our postulate. Numbers are fictitious.

We will test the DLCCS by estimating the probability of an increase or decrease in M_T (total money supply) occurring at a 75 percent to ∞ confidence levels.

Our model is based on the economic fundamentals of an unidentified country member of the Eurozone. We do realize of course that countries in the Eurozone have different economic fundamentals; however the principle is the same, and we do not believe the process portrayed in this model referred to a hypothetical member country would be so much different in the aggregate. In the example we have used the exchange rate for Drachmas when they were converted into Euros, namely, 340 Drachmas (in round numbers) to one Euro. Time horizon is 12 months.

The total money supply has been converted to Solids, and the values of random events were calculated as a percentage of the base value, that is, of the total money supply. The probability of a devaluation increases from 60% to 80% if the total money supply is expanded. This condition has been entered as a cascade risk effect in the model.

INCREASE IN LOCAL MONEY SUPPLY (M_{LC})
Probability of occurring: 40%
Distribution: betaPERT with the following money supply expansion values: 20% Min, 21% Mode, 22% Max

LOCAL CURRENCY IS DEVALUED
Probability of occurring: 60%
Distribution: betaPERT with the following devaluation values: -14% Min, -13% Mode, -12% Max

NET INCOME DUE TO POSITIVE BALANCE OF TRADE
Probability of occurring: 30%
Distribution: betaPERT with the following values: 5% Min, 6% Mode, 7% Max

NET INVESTMENT (Balance of Payments) Probability of occurring: 20%
Distribution: betaPERT with the following values: 10% Min, 11% Mode, 12% Max

PRIVATE GOLD IS EXCHANGED FOR SOLIDS
Probability of occurring: 40%
Distribution: betaPERT with the following values: 15% Min, 16% Mode, 17% Max

Below is the table with the details:

ASSUMPTIONS	Millions	In Solids
Money supply – Solids (M_S)	1,000	1,000
Money supply – Local Currency M_{LC}	500,000	1,471
Total money supply (M_T		2,471

RANDOM EVENTS	PROBABIL.	MIN	MAX	MAX
Increase in M_{LC}	40%	$294	309	$324
Local currency is devalued	60%	-$206	-$191	-$176
Income due to PBT	30%	$50	$60	$70
Net Investment	20%	$100	$110	$120
Priv. Gold Exc. For Solids	40%	$150	$160	$170

M_{LC}: Local currency
PBT: Positive balance of trade

We run 50,000 samples simulating the operation of the economy and obtain the following result at a 75% confidence level:

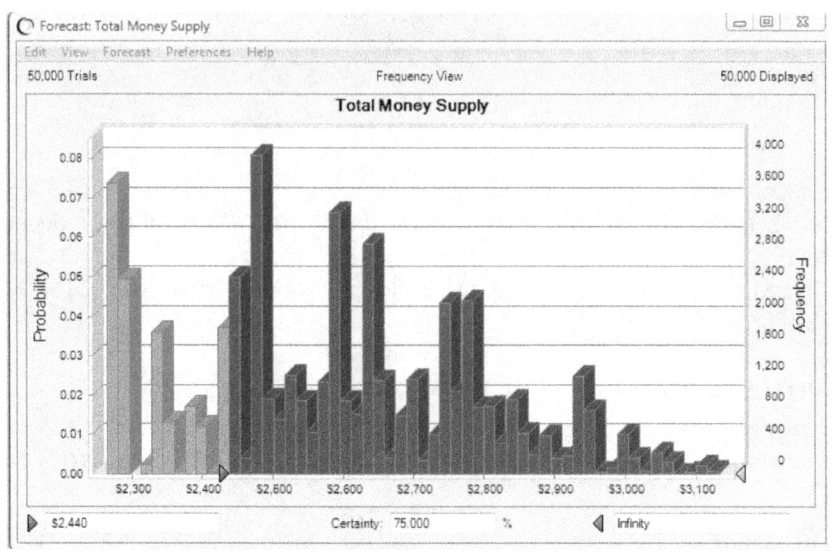

The result indicates that after factoring in all the random events, there is a probability of 75% to ∞ that the total value supply will be at least $2,440 billion of Solids. Hence, it also means that the total money supply could end up being slightly lower than the initial value of $2,471 billion Solids. Under the DLCCS, the government may decide to increase the local money supply or even better, issue bonds denominated in dollars for example, to be used to purchase gold and convert it into Solid, to make up for the shortfall.

The government may even simulate possible scenarios before expanding the money supply in the local currency to learn the possible impact in the total money supply expressed in Solids. This can of course be done by applying stochastic processes in the form of quantitative risk analysis, creating a much more complex model that the one exhibited above.

We would like to emphasize once more, that the objective of creating this very simple stochastic simulation model was to simply illustrate the way in which the economy would work under a Dual-Level Currency Competition System. A much more complex model could certainly be built.

11 CONCLUSIONS

The history of the informed quest for a monetary system that works long-term has been going on for about two and a half centuries. the problem encountered is not necessarily the ignorance about what to do in order to have money that is not ravished by inflation or the cause of deflation. The reality is that the real problem has always had to do with the ideological corruption and an exceedingly high level of incompetence from the part of politicians and economists, who bent and broke the rules rendering any monetary system moot. A watershed in this downhill process was the Peel Act of 1884 which monopolized the note issue in England and signaled the progressive deterioration of money. The nationalization of money was somehow disguised as a measure to "bring order into monetary affairs" when in reality it had much more to do with enabling politicians' arbitrary spending to finance a great variety of follies and political adventures, including wars. This has brought all kinds of misfortunes upon the population, arbitrary suspensions of the gold standard, devaluations of the *fiat* currencies, economic and political crisis, at both national and international levels.

The fact is that the above is simply the reality and it makes little sense ignoring it, pushing it aside and hoping that a strict, inflexible monetary system like the gold standard will work long-term, uncorrupted. Others may hope that competent, uncorrupted politicians —ideologically speaking and otherwise— will lay down a set of policies that will bring a renaissance to the way monetary systems are managed and respected. Experience has shown this to be an unadulterated *Fata Morgana* worthy of *Morgan la Fay* herself.

In this essay we have described the framework of a monetary system which takes into account human failings which is unequivocally at the very core of the problem. Our DLCCS-Dual Level Currency Competition System allows the "tampering" of the system which however must necessarily be moderate, due to its self-regulating (by human action) feature. The DLCCS possesses the capacity of self-regulation with a built-in tendency of returning to monetary discipline. The system is not perfect; no system is. However we believe it to be vastly superior to any other monetary system known, current or past.

It is also to be emphasized that the DLCCS would be well suited to a continent like Latin America; as a matter of fact it would be very well suited to be introduced as a monetary system to the world.

Finally, we believe that the best way we can sum up our conclusions in a concise manner is by specifically answering some of the main questions posed in relation to the situation created by the hypothetical case of one or more members exiting the Eurozone.

How to ensure that any new currencies would be stable?
The Solid will have a 100 percent reserve in gold which is the strongest guarantee a country can have to separate politics from honest money. The reissuance of local currencies will avail governments the possibility of expanding the local currency supply of money thus extracting resources from society. However, this expansion must necessarily be moderate and short lived; otherwise it will cause the dumping of the local currency in favor of the Solid, denying governments the collection of the inflation tax.

What areas should the new currencies cover?
The Solid will circulate in all the countries members of the Eurozone, side-by-side with the reissued local currencies.

In what currency would government debt be paid back?
Debts denominated in Euros will be paid back in Solids and/or in the local currency at the prevailing exchange rate. The amount paid either in Solids or in a mixture of Solids and local currency will amount to the original face value of the debt in Euros.

What happens to individuals' debts? say you live in Greece and your wages are changed into new Drachma, and your mortgage with a Spanish bank is in Euros? The question is, do you have to pay that back in Euros or does it change to being paid in the new currency?
The answer is that this scenario will simply not occur under the DLCCS monetary system we are proposing. The procedure will be the same as for government debt as outlined above. under the DLCCS, neither creditors nor debtors will suffer losses.

This booklet was sent for publishing before the 17th may 2012 Greek elections.

REFERENCES

1. Friedrich A. Hayek, Choice in Currency: A Way to Stop Inflation. The Institute of Economic Affairs . Occasional Paper 48.

London1976 Denationalization of Money: The Argument Refined. The Institute of Economic Affairs. London 1978.

2. Eduardo J. Belgrano."Can the Euro-Monetary Symphony Play in Tune?" The News, Mexico August 25, 1997.

3. http://www.smh.com.au/world/desperate-families-give-up-children-as-greeces-financial-crisis-hits-home-20111229-1pe97.html

4. Emil-Maria Claassen. Europäische Währungsunion: Einige Anmerkungen zum Konzept der Parallelwährung. 1977

5. http://2012indyinfo.com/2011/12/03/jacques-delors-euro-was-flawed-from-beginning/

6.http://www.reuters.com/article/2011/12/19/us-ecb-highlights-idUSTRE7BI18T20111219

7. Vera C. Smith „The Rationale of Central Banking" 1932

8. http://blogs.wsj.com/brussels/2011/05/09/luxembourg-lies-on-secret-meeting/

9. http://www.businessweek.com/magazine/germanys-hidden-risk-12142011.html#

10. Phillip Cagan. Would the Gold Standard Help?, Studies in Contemporary Economic Problems, 1982. Page 23

11. Roy W. Jastram. The Gold Standard: You Can't Trust Politics. Wall Street Journal. 15 May 1981. P.32.

12. John H. Williams, The Crisis of the Gold Standard. 1932- P. 392-393 – Foreign Affairs

13. Truman A. Clark. Violations of the Gold Points 1890-1908. Journal of Political Economy. Volume 92 Number 4 August 1984

14. Robert A. Mundell. Theory of Optimal Currency Areas.

15. Robert A. Mundell. "A Theory of Optimum Currency Areas". 1961. The Economics of Integration P.179

16. Peter Kenen. „The Theory of Optimum Currency Areas: An Eclectic View" 1969. P.48

17. Alexandre Kafka. „Optimum Currency Areas and Latin America". 1973 P. 212

18. http://bigthink.com/ideas/21182

19. Wolfram Engels, Frankfurt Die Realassetwährung -Währungsmonopol bei Notenemissionskonkurrenz,. - Geldordnung u. Geldpolitik, Mohr, Tübingen 1982 S. 35-43 JZL –. "Konkurrenz zwischen Währungen – sog. Parallelwährungen – hat es in der Geschichte nur vereinzelt und über ganz kurze Zeiträume gegeben." P. 42

20. Roland Vaubel. Strategies for Currency Unification. Kieler Studien. IWW. Kiel. 1978. P. 362.

21 Chau Nan Chen, "Flexible Bimetallic Exchange Rates in China 1650-1850". Journal of Money, Credit and Banking, Vol 7, 1975

22. Eduardo J. Belgrano. "Latin Lesson". Economic Affairs, Institute of Economic Affairs. September 1991. London.

23. http://www.scielo.org.bo/pdf/rlde/v7n12/v7n12a02.pdf

24. Benjamin Klein. The Competitive Supply of Money. 1974. Page 449

25.. Eduardo J. Belgrano. „Inflacion Cero. Un Objetivo Posible y Alcanzable a Corto Plazo". Index Economico. Banco de Análisis y Computación. Buenos Aires. July 1985. Ano VII. Vol. 8

26. Thomas Guggenheim. „Some early Views on Monetary Integration" in The Economics of Common Currencies. 1973.

27. Karl Helfferich, Das Geld (Leipzig: C. L. Hirschfeld, 1923 [1910]), p. 646

ABOUT THE AUTHOR

The author studied business administration and economics at an undergraduate and graduate level, and has held senior positions in companies in various countries. He is an international consultant in the fields of business and economics and has lived in eight different countries for reasons of study and work. While providing consulting for one of the biggest mining groups in Bolivia, he had a firsthand experience in the effects of hyperinflation on the population which developed in the country in 1985, at that time the biggest in the world occurring since the Hungarian hyperinflation in 1945.

He has lectured at universities and institutions on the subject of economics and business, and has written articles in specialized magazines and newspapers in various countries.

The author currently provides consulting in the area of quantitative risk analysis referred to the fields of strategic planning, builds risk scenarios of assets exposed to risk for clients such as oil companies, and also consults on the business cycle.

www.ingramcontent.com/pod-product-compliance
Lightning Source LLC
Chambersburg PA
CBHW071635170526
45166CB00003B/1330